HAUNTINGS

By John Hawkins

PowerKiDS
press

New York

Published in 2012 by The Rosen Publishing Group, Inc.
29 East 21st Street, New York, NY 10010

Author: John Hawkins
Editor and Picture Researcher: Joe Harris
U.S. Editor: Kara Murray
Design: Emma Randall
Cover Design: Emma Randall

Picture credits:
Art Archive/Kobal: 8. Corbis: 1, 4, 6, 7, 11, 12, 13, 15, 16, 18, 19, 24, 27, 28, 29, 32. Getty: 22. Mary Evans: 14,
17, 20, 21, 25, 26. Science Photo Library: 5. Shutterstock: cover, 9, 23. TopFoto: 10.

Library of Congress Cataloging-in-Publication Data

Hawkins, John.
 Hauntings / by John Hawkins.
    p. cm. — (Mystery hunters)
 Includes index.
 ISBN 978-1-4488-6428-7 (library binding) — ISBN 978-1-4488-6439-3 (pbk.) —
 ISBN 978-1-4488-6440-9 (6-pack)
 1. Ghosts—Juvenile literature. I. Title.
 BF1461.H39 2012
 133.109—dc23

                          2011019428

Printed in China

SL002065US

CPSIA Compliance Information: Batch #AW2102PK: For Further Information contact Rosen Publishing, New York, New York at 1-800-237-9932

CONTENTS

Ancient Apparitions.. 4

Fateful Appearances.. 6

Ghosts of War... 8

Living Apparitions 10

Talking to the Dead 12

Possession 14

The Bloody Tower... 16

The Ghosts of Glamis 18

Noises in the Night 20

Tombstone... 22

Versailles.. 24

Borley Rectory 26

Alcatraz... 28

Glossary.. 30

Further Reading and Web Sites........................... 31

Index 32

ANCIENT APPARITIONS

The belief in an immortal human soul and its survival after death dates back to prehistoric times and is common to almost every culture around the world.

A WOMAN WRONGED

According to a Japanese folk story, there once lived a samurai who believed his wife had been unfaithful to him. In a jealous rage he disfigured her, slicing at her face, and said, "Who will think you're beautiful now?"

▲ *This eighteenth-century Japanese painting, by Maruyama Okyo, shows a man terrified when his own ghostly painting comes to life.*

BACK FROM THE DEAD

Ever since that day, the spirit of that woman has been found wandering through the fog, her face covered with a mask. She is known as Kuchisake-onna, which translates as "Slit-Mouthed Woman." When she meets young men and women, she asks "*Watashi kirei*?" "Am I beautiful?" If they answer "yes" she tears off the mask, revealing the true horror of her face, and asks again. If people keep

EXAMINING THE EVIDENCE

ARE GHOSTS REAL?

The witnesses whose stories have been told in this book were probably telling the truth, and believed they experienced something supernatural. But could their senses have been deceiving them? Sometimes ghostly apparitions can be explained by people seeing unusual reflections or shadows or hearing strange echoes. Noises below the range of human hearing can make people feel that someone else is in the room with them. Scientists have also suggested that some "haunted" houses may have unusual magnetic fields, which can trigger hallucinations. However science cannot prove that ghosts definitely do not exist.

their nerve and again answer "yes," she allows them to go on their way.

However if they answer truthfully by saying "no," or try to flee from her, she pursues them, brandishing a scythe. If she catches a man, he's as good as dead. However if she catches a woman, she may turn her into another Kuchisake-onna, doomed to wander the world as a spirit of vengeance.

▶ Many people believe that we have not just a physical body, but also a spiritual body which can live after death.

FATEFUL APPEARANCES

According to some stories, ghosts of the recently departed occasionally appear to relatives in order to pass on important messages.

BIBLICAL MESSAGE

In 1925, James Chaffin of Davie County, North Carolina, dreamed that his dead father urged him to look for his missing will in the pocket of the overcoat that he was wearing in the dream. James found the coat with his brother John. In the lining of the inside pocket they found a message in his father's handwriting. It told them to read Genesis 27 in the family Bible. They opened the Bible to the first page of that chapter, and there was the missing will.

▼ James Chaffin was told to read the twenty-seventh chapter of Genesis in the Bible.

▲ *This illustration by Robert Dunley (published 1856–1858) shows Shakespeare's Hamlet being approached by the ghost of his murdered father.*

bed, dressed in a naval officer's uniform. She woke her husband. He recognized the intruder as his father, who had died several years earlier. The ghost simply spoke his son's name and walked through the facing wall.

FATHER'S WARNING

The Society of Psychical Research reported a story about a woman, "Mrs. P.," who one night saw a stranger standing at the foot of her

The husband later confessed to his wife that he had accumulated a large debt and was so desperate that he had been thinking of going into business with a dishonest character. He took his father's appearance as a warning and was now determined to solve his financial difficulties by himself.

STRANGE STORIES
Garment gift

American farmer Michael Conley passed away in 1885. When his daughter was informed of his death, she fainted. On recovering, she claimed that her father had appeared to her and told her to recover a roll of dollar bills he had sewn into the lining of his gray shirt. She said he'd wrapped the money in a square of red cloth. No one believed her, but they agreed to get the clothes from the morgue. In the lining of the gray shirt, wrapped in a patch of red cloth, was a roll of dollar bills.

GHOSTS OF WAR

During the World War I, both the Germans and the Allies reported several sightings of ghostly soldiers who intervened to save the lives of their comrades.

▲ *It was a popular legend by 1914 that a host of angels had helped to repel a German advance in World War I.*

SPECTRAL SOLDIER

In November 1916, British soldiers were defending their trench against a German attack when they apparently saw the white figure of a soldier rise out of a shell hole and walk slowly along the front, oblivious to shells and bullets. It then turned toward the Germans, and they scattered.

The same phantom figure was seen later by a British officer, William Speight, in his dugout. It pointed to a spot on the dugout floor, then vanished. Speight ordered a hole to be dug on the spot. To his amazement, the diggers unearthed a tunnel excavated by the Germans, primed with mines timed to explode 13 hours later.

EYEWITNESS TO MYSTERY
SAYING GOOD-BYE

World War I soldier and poet Wilfred Owen was killed a week before the war ended. His brother Harold, a naval officer, described his final "meeting" with him on Armistice Day. At the time, Harold didn't know his brother was already dead.

". . . to my amazement I saw Wilfred sitting in my chair. . . I felt shock run through me with appalling force. . . I spoke quietly: 'Wilfred how did you get here?' He did not rise and I saw that he was involuntarily immobile, but. . . when I spoke his whole face broke into his sweetest and endearing dark smile. . . I must have turned my eyes away from him; when I looked back my cabin chair was empty."

▼ *Belief in automatic writing was fashionable in Victorian London. Spiritualists believed that a spirit could control a person's writing hand to send a message.*

SPOOKY SCRIPT

Sir Arthur Conan Doyle, creator of Sherlock Holmes, had an acquaintance, Lily Loder-Symonds, who believed that spirits could write through her. To Conan Doyle's astonishment, Loder-Symonds one day began writing in the style of his late brother-in-law Malcolm Leckie, who had been killed at the battle of Mons in 1915. Conan Doyle asked "Malcolm" questions that he believed only his brother-in-law could have answered. All were answered accurately.

LIVING APPARITIONS

It's a well-known theory that ghosts are the spirits of the dead. But some people believe that living people can also have a ghostly double.

▲ Many people believe that it is possible for living people to appear in one location while they are elsewhere.

TWO PLACES AT ONCE

Emilie Sagee was a teacher at a girls' school in Livonia in 1845. Although capable and conscientious, there was something odd about her. Rumors spread that she was often seen in two parts of the school simultaneously. On one occasion, a class of 13 saw Miss Sagee standing with her doppelgänger at the blackboard.

One morning, the entire school was in a classroom overlooking the garden where Miss Sagee could be seen picking flowers. Suddenly, her double appeared in a chair in the classroom. Outside, her movements grew sluggish. According to witnesses, two of the girls touched the double and their hands passed right through it. Moments later, the double faded and Miss Sagee began moving normally again.

PHANTOM FORERUNNER

Businessman Erkson Gorique visited Norway for the first time in July 1955—or did he? When he checked into his hotel the clerk said: "It's good to have you back, Mr. Gorique." The next day, Gorique introduced himself to a potential customer and was greeted like an old acquaintance. Mystified, Gorique assured the man it was his first visit. The customer just smiled. "This is not so unusual here in Norway," he said. "In fact, it happens so often we have a name for it. We call it the *vardoger,* or forerunner."

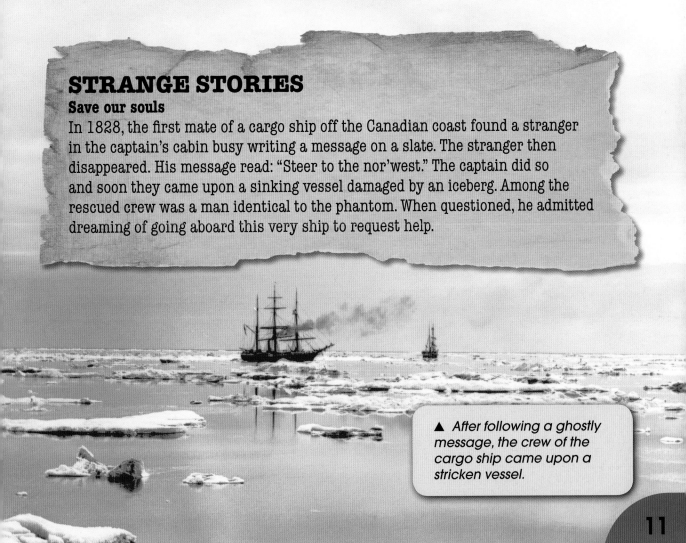

STRANGE STORIES
Save our souls
In 1828, the first mate of a cargo ship off the Canadian coast found a stranger in the captain's cabin busy writing a message on a slate. The stranger then disappeared. His message read: "Steer to the nor'west." The captain did so and soon they came upon a sinking vessel damaged by an iceberg. Among the rescued crew was a man identical to the phantom. When questioned, he admitted dreaming of going aboard this very ship to request help.

▲ After following a ghostly message, the crew of the cargo ship came upon a stricken vessel.

TALKING TO THE DEAD

Psychic mediums claim to have a heightened sensitivity to the subtle forces and presences around us. This, they say, enables them to act as a channel between the living and the dead.

BETTY SHINE

Celebrity psychic Betty Shine said that she obtained her "powers" in an unusual way. As a young evacuee during World War II, her house was struck by a stray bomb, which blew in the windows and sent a shard of glass into the headboard just above her head. The following night, Betty began seeing "misty people" passing through the room. She soon realized that they were spirits of the dead.

▼ *Séances are attempts by living people to contact the spirits of the dead.*

Some religious people believe that using Ouija boards can be dangerous. ▶

TINA HAMILTON

Catholic sacristan Tina Hamilton lives in Canterbury, England. She says that she often senses the presence of spirits. Once she encountered the confused spirit of a young man who had been killed in a car accident. She said he kept reliving the crash like a bad dream and couldn't accept he hadn't survived it.

MYSTERY BELL

Psychic John Edward says that messages can be hard to interpret. One male spirit kept showing him a bell. What could it mean? The man's bereaved wife said that just before his death, her husband had given her a souvenir bell as a gift.

? FACT HUNTER

OUIJA BOARD

What is it? A board printed with letters, to which a planchette (movable indicator) points, to allow communication with the dead

Invented by: The Fuld brothers of Baltimore in 1898

How does it work? Participants place their finger on the planchette and wait for spirits to move it to spell out answers to their questions

Possible explanation: Involuntary muscle contractions in participants' hands known as ideomotor actions

POSSESSION

Some people believe that dead souls can take over the bodies of the living. It sounds scary, but they say it can be for a benign purpose, as in the case of Lurancy Vennum.

THE VENNUM CASE

At the age of 13, Lurancy Vennum from Watseka, Illinois, fell into a trance during which she claimed to be Mary Roff, a neighbor girl who had died when Lurancy was a year old. She asked if she could go "home," and the Roffs agreed to take

▲ Lurancy appeared to be taken over completely by the spirit of "Mary."

her in. Lurancy as "Mary" recognized the furnishings in the house, and identified many of Mary's prized possessions. She even greeted Mary's old Sunday school teacher by name. She was able to answer many personal questions thrown at her by the Roffs, including details of a family holiday and where a pet dog died.

EXAMINING THE EVIDENCE

WAS LURANCY GENUINE?

The Lurancy case was reviewed by psychologist Frank Hoffmann. He said that the grieving Roff family encouraged Lurancy to believe that she was Mary. Another investigator, Henry Bruce, pointed out that the "Mary personality" only appeared when the Roffs were present and disappeared entirely upon Lurancy's marriage.

RETURNING SPIRITS

John and Florence Pollock were heartbroken when their daughters, Joanna and Jacqueline, were killed in a car crash in Hexham, England, in 1957. Two years later, Florence gave birth to twin girls. The girls grew up in a different town, but when they were three they were taken back to Hexham. The girls recognized the family's former home, the school, and places where their sisters used to play. At age four, they were given their dead sisters' toy box and could identify all the dolls by name. Disturbingly, they seemed to remember being run over by a car. Their parents had never told them about the accident. Were they reincarnations of their sisters? Some, including their father, were sure of it.

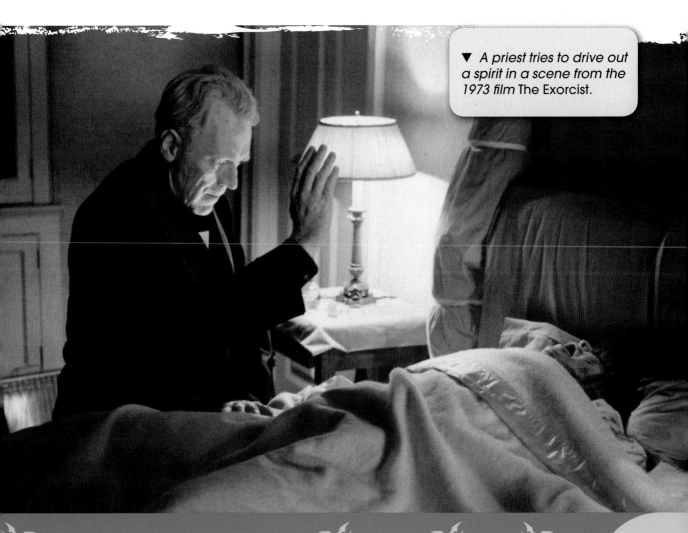

▼ *A priest tries to drive out a spirit in a scene from the 1973 film* The Exorcist.

THE BLOODY TOWER

If any site deserves its reputation for spectral sightings it is the Tower of London, whose weathered stones are soaked in the blood of countless executed martyrs and traitors.

THE TWO PRINCES

In 1483, Princes Edward and Richard of England may have been murdered by their ambitious uncle the Duke of Gloucester, the future Richard III, so that he could become king. No one knows the truth, but the two boys have been seen on several occasions, walking through the tower's chilly corridors at dusk.

GHOSTLY PURSUIT

The Countess of Salisbury, Margaret Pole, was 70 years old when she was condemned to death for treason in 1541. Standing regally on the

▼ *The Tower of London on the Thames River.*

▲ *Does the ghost of Anne Boleyn still roam the Tower today?*

head where she stood. When he refused, she fled, and was killed after a bloody chase. It is said that after dark, on the anniversary of her death, this gruesome scene is reenacted, as Pole's ghost tries once again to outrun her executioner.

THE PHANTOM QUEEN

Lady Jane Grey was just 15 years old when she became queen in 1553. She ruled for only nine days, before being arrested and condemned to death. She was beheaded on Tower Hill on February 12, 1554. Since then, her ghost has been seen by witnesses on several occasions. In 1957, two sentries swore they witnessed the apparition of the young queen on the roof of the Salt Tower.

scaffold, she refused to kneel for the executioner. Instead she commanded him to sever her

STRANGE STORIES
Anne Boleyn
Anne Boleyn, the second wife of Henry VIII, was beheaded in 1536. Startled visitors have reported seeing her lead a spectral procession through the Tower Chapel, where she made her final prayers, sometimes with and sometimes without her head.

THE GHOSTS OF GLAMIS

Glamis Castle in Scotland is the ancestral home of the late Queen Mother Elizabeth Bowes-Lyon. It also has the unenviable reputation as the most haunted castle in the world.

CASTLE LEGENDS

Several visitors claim to have seen a pale, frightened young girl pleading in mute terror at a barred window. Legend has it she had her tongue cut out for betraying a family secret.

In 1537, the widow of the sixth Lord Glamis was burned for witchcraft. It is said that ever since, on the anniversary of her death, her ghost has been seen on the roof of the clock tower, bathed in a smoldering red glow.

▼ *Glamis Castle*

In the 1920s, a workman was said to have accidentally uncovered a hidden passage and to have been driven to the edge of insanity by what he found there. Allegedly the family bought his silence by paying for him to move to another country.

GHOSTLY FIGURE

In 1869, a guest named Mrs. Munro was awoken in the night by the sensation of someone bending over her. She may even have felt a beard brush her face. The night-light had gone out, so she told her husband to get up and find the matches. In the moonlight, she saw a figure pass into the dressing room. Creeping to the end of the bed, she felt for and found the matchbox.

▲ A man appears to be startled by a white-garbed ghost in this photograph from 1910.

She lit one and called out loudly, "Cam, Cam, I've found the matches." To her surprise she saw that her husband hadn't moved from her side. There was no one in the room.

EYEWITNESS TO MYSTERY
DEATH'S DOOR
Scottish novelist Sir Walter Scott braved a night at Glamis in 1793 and lived to regret it, "I must own, that when I heard door after door shut, after my conductor had retired, I began to consider myself as too far from the living, and somewhat too near the dead."

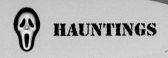
NOISES IN THE NIGHT

During the spring of 1848, the Fox family of Hydesville, New York, claimed that their nights were disturbed by strange noises. The family slept in the same room, so all apparently witnessed the noises.

COMMUNICATING WITH THE DEAD

On the evening of March 31, Mrs. Fox and her children Margaretta and Kate were in bed when they heard a loud rapping. Kate assumed someone was playing a practical joke. She challenged whomever it was to copy her. She snapped her fingers and was immediately answered by the same number of raps. Mrs. Fox asked out

▼ *The Fox family responding to mysterious rappings in their home in Hydesville, New York, as illustrated in literature of the time.*

loud if it was a human being making the noises. There was no reply. "Is it a spirit?" she asked. "If it is, make two raps." She was answered emphatically with two bangs that shook the house.

MURDER MOST FOUL

Mrs. Fox developed a simple code to communicate with the spirit, and the intruder (so she claimed) told her that it was the spirit of a 31-year-old man who had been murdered in the house. A neighbor by the name of William Duesler was invited into the room. Using Mrs. Fox's code, Duesler discovered that the murdered man was a peddler by the name of Charles Rosma, who had been killed five years earlier by a previous tenant of the house, a Mr. Bell, for the $500 he had saved and carried with him. When the murdered man informed the family

▲ The Fox sisters Margaretta (left) and Kate (center) with their older sister, Leah, who had left home at the time of the haunting.

that his body had been buried in their cellar, Mr. Fox immediately started digging up the dirt floor. He discovered human bone fragments 5 feet (1.5 m) down.

EYEWITNESS TO MYSTERY
TESTING THE TAPPER
Mrs. Fox later wrote: "I then thought I could put a test that no one in the place could answer. I asked the noise to rap my different children's ages, successively. Instantly, each one of my children's ages was given correctly."

TOMBSTONE

They called Tombstone, Arizona, the town too tough to die and, according to the stories, some of its most notorious inhabitants are equally reluctant to go quietly.

GHOST TOWN

The town is now preserved as a national museum with many of the old buildings restored to their former rickety glory. Some say that if you stay in the bar after closing time, you can hear the honky-tonk piano playing "Red River Valley" and hear the cowboys' raucous laughter.

SALOON SPECTERS

The meanest gunfighters of the Old West drank and gambled at the town's Bird Cage Theater, which doubled as

▼ This photo of Tombstone dates from 1885. The town suffered two major fires in 1881 and 1882. By the mid-1880s, the place was virtually abandoned.

a saloon. According to tour guides, 31 ghosts haunt the saloon, which was the site of 26 killings. The phantom most frequently seen is a stagehand dressed in black striped pants.

▼ Violent deaths were not uncommon in the Old West.

WOMAN IN WHITE

Saloon staff say that objects such as poker chips regularly appear and disappear and furniture moves by itself. One member of the staff said he was physically attacked by a spirit. A woman working in the gift shop swears she once saw on a security monitor a woman in a white dress walking through the cellar.

STRANGE STORIES
The ghost of Boot Hill Cemetery

In 1996, Terry Ike Clanton took a photo of his friend at Tombstone's cemetery on Boot Hill. When Clanton had the photo developed, he was startled to see among the gravestones, just to the right of his friend, a thin man in a dark hat. The man appears to be legless and kneeling or rising up out of the ground. Clanton is confident there was no one else in the shot when he took the picture. Unlike his friend, the man casts no shadow.

VERSAILLES

On August 10, 1901, two English women, Miss Moberly and Miss Jourdain, were visiting the French palace of Versailles, where Louis XVI and his queen Marie Antoinette lived just prior to the French Revolution. Neither Miss Moberly nor Miss Jourdain believed in the paranormal. What they claimed to have experienced that day was enough to change their minds.

▲ Marie Antoinette depicted by Elisabeth Vigee-Lebrun in 1783

GLIMPSING THE PAST

While strolling through the formal gardens, the women lost their way. At the edge of a wood they saw a pillared kiosk. Seated there was a man in a cloak with malevolent features. As the ladies debated which direction to take, a handsome young man in a wide-brimmed hat appeared. Following his directions, they found themselves at the Petit Trianon, Marie Antoinette's private chateau. Seated there was a pretty, fair-haired young woman in period costume, sketching.

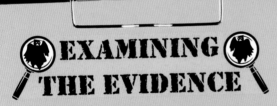

▼ *You can see the crowd at the execution of Marie Antoinette in this eighteenth-century Danish School painting.*

RESEARCH

The women later discovered that August 10 was the day that revolutionaries marched on Versailles and seized the royal family. Had they tapped into a residual memory of that event?

They looked at historic documents and saw there had been a pillared kiosk there at that time. The malevolent-looking man answered to the description of Comte de Vaudreuil, who had betrayed the queen. The handsome young man looked like the messenger who hurried to warn her of the mob marching on the palace. And the young woman could have been Marie Antoinette herself.

EXAMINING THE EVIDENCE

DID THEY REALLY EXPERIENCE HISTORY?

Skeptics have argued that the women mistook actors in period costume for genuine specters. In fact the poet Robert de Montesquieu records that he and his friends often amused themselves by dressing in period costume and wandering the grounds of Versailles. However, this does not explain how the women saw the kiosk, which had vanished by 1901.

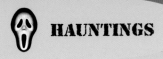

BORLEY RECTORY

During the 1930s and 1940s, Borley Rectory became known as the most haunted house in England. This vicarage near Sudbury, Essex, was built on the site of a monastery. It is said that a Borley monk fell in love with a local nun. They were caught together and the monk was executed. The nun was walled up alive in the cellar.

FIRST SIGHTINGS

The first resident of the new rectory was the Reverend Bull, who often observed the weeping nun wandering his garden in search of her lost love.

▼ Bones were found in the cellar of the rectory and, in an effort to quiet the ghost, given a decent burial in Liston churchyard in 1945.

▼ *The ruins of Borley Rectory at the start of its demolition. A brick flies through the air (circled below). Is this a paranormal event?*

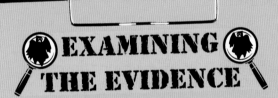

GHOST HUNTER

In 1929, Reverend Eric Smith and his wife moved in and were immediately confronted by poltergeist activity. They decided to call in a ghost hunter, Harry Price. He recorded incidents involving phantom footsteps, flying objects, and even physical attacks. Unintelligible messages were scrawled on the walls, servants' bells rang of their own accord, and music could be heard coming from the chapel while it was empty.

BURNED DOWN

The Smiths left after just two years, and their successors did not last much longer. The house burned down in a mysterious fire in 1939.

EXAMINING THE EVIDENCE

DID PRICE FAKE THE EVIDENCE?

Harry Price made his name with a best-selling book about Borley, but skeptics raised questions. They said that Price, a former stage magician, faked certain phenomena. Yet the Bull family claimed the house was haunted before Price moved in. Even if Price was a fraud, it seems that there may have been something genuinely mysterious going on at Borley Rectory.

ALCATRAZ

Long before Alcatraz Island in San Francisco Bay was converted into a prison, Native Americans warned the U.S. army not to build a fortress on what was called the Rock as it was the dwelling place of evil spirits.

DEMON EYES

When the fortress was converted into a military prison in 1912, several soldiers were said to have been driven insane by mysterious noises in the night, by cold spots that turned their breath to mist, and by the sight of burning red eyes that appeared in the lower-level cells. Even the most hardened inmates feared being thrown into "the hole," the windowless cells of D Block where the red-eyed demon was said to dwell.

▼ According to Native American beliefs, the Rock was the dwelling place of evil spirits, and anyone living there was in peril.

▼ Other parts of the prison are supposedly host to the unquiet spirits of the five suicides and eight murders which took place before the prison was closed in 1963.

STRANGE STORIES
Mystery of 14D

On one memorable night during the 1940s, a prisoner was hurled screaming into solitary in 14D and continued yelling all night. When the guards finally opened his cell, they found him dead, with distinctive marks around his throat. The official cause of death was given as "non-self-inflicted strangulation."

The next morning, the prisoners were lined up for roll call, but the number was wrong. There was one extra prisoner in the line. A guard walked along the line to see if an inmate was playing a trick on him. He later claimed that he came face to face with the dead man, who promptly vanished before his eyes.

JAILHOUSE JITTERS

The ghosts of prisoners who died attempting to escape are said to haunt the hospital block where their bodies were taken. Other parts of the prison are host to the unquiet spirits of the five suicides and eight murders which took place before the prison was closed in 1963. Since the Rock opened to tourists, visitors have claimed to have heard the sound of sobbing, moaning, and phantom footsteps.

GLOSSARY

ancestral (an-SES-trul) Belonging to and inherited from one's ancestors.

apparition (a-puh-RIH-shun) A ghost.

automatic writing (aw-tuh-MA-tik RYT-ing) Writing said to be produced by a spiritual or subconscious agency rather than by the conscious intention of the writer.

benign (bih-NYN) Gentle, kind, and well-intentioned.

doppelgänger (DO-pel-gang-er) An apparition or double of a living person.

evacuee (ih-va-kyuh-WEE) A person taken from a place of danger to somewhere safe.

excavated (EK-skuh-vayt-ed) Made a hole by digging.

forerunner (FAWR-ruh-ner) A person or thing that precedes the coming of someone or something else.

immobile (im-MOH-bel) Not moving.

intervened (in-ter-VEEND) Came between so as to prevent or alter a course of events.

kiosk (KEE-osk) An open pavilion.

malevolent (muh-LEH-vuh-lent) Having or showing a wish to do evil to others.

martyrs (MAR-terz) People who are killed for their beliefs.

mediums (MEE-dee-umz) People claiming to be in contact with the spirits of the dead and to communicate between the dead and the living.

non-self-inflicted strangulation (non-self-in-FLIKT-ed strang-gyuh-LAY-shun) Being strangled by someone or something other than oneself.

peddler (PED-lur) A person who goes from place to place selling small goods.

planchette (plan-SHET) A small board supported on casters, typically heart shaped and fitted with a vertical pencil, used with a Ouija board and also for automatic writing and séances.

poltergeist (POHL-ter-gyst) A ghost or other supernatural being supposedly responsible for physical disturbances such as loud noises and objects thrown around.

psychologist (sy-KAH-luh-jist) An expert in psychology, the study of the human mind and its functions.

reincarnations (ree-in-kar-NAY-shenz) Rebirths of souls in new bodies.

residual (rih-ZIH-juh-wul) Remaining after the greater part or quantity has gone.

roll call (ROHL KAWL) The process of calling out to establish how many people are present.

sacristan (SA-kruh-stun) A person in charge of a sacristy (a room in a church where a priest prepares for a service and where vestments and other things used in worship are kept).

samurai (SA-muh-ry) A member of a powerful military class in feudal Japan.

scythe (SYTH) A tool with a long, curved blade, used for cutting crops.

specter (SPEK-ter) A ghost.

spectral (SPEK-trul) Of or like a ghost.

trance (TRANTS) A mental state in which a person is not aware of the world around them.

FURTHER READING

Doak, Robin S. *Investigating Hauntings, Ghosts, and Poltergeists*. Unexplained Phenomena. Mankato, MN: Capstone Press, 2011.

Malam, John. *Ghosts*. Monster Mania. Philadelphia, PA: QED Publishing, 2010.

Matthews, Rupert. *Ghosts and Spirits*. Unexplained. Philadelphia, PA: QED Publishing, 2011.

Miles, Liz. *Terrifying Tales: Ghosts, Ghouls and Other Things That Go Bump in the Night*. Culture in Action. Mankato, MN: Heinemann Raintree, 2010.

WEB SITES

Due to the changing nature of Internet links, PowerKids Press has developed an online list of Web sites related to the subject of this book. This site is updated regularly. Please use this link to access the list:

www.powerkidslinks.com/mysthunt/haunt/

INDEX

Alcatraz Island 28
apparition 4–5, 10, 17
automatic writing 9

Borley Rectory 26–27

castle 18

death 4–5, 7, 13, 16–19,
    23, 29
doppelgänger 10

evidence 5, 14, 25, 27
execution 17, 25
eyewitness 9, 19, 21

footsteps 27, 29

ghost(s) 5–8, 10, 17–19,
    23, 26, 29
ghost hunter 27
ghost town 22
Glamis Castle 18–19

house 5, 12, 14, 21, 26–27

mask 4
mediums 12
message(s) 6, 9, 11, 13, 27
murder 7, 16, 21, 29

Native Americans 28
noises 5, 20–21, 28
nun 26

Ouija board 13

palace of Versailles 24–25
phantom 8, 11, 17, 23,
    27, 29
poltergeist 27
possession 14–15
prehistoric 4
priest 15
psychic 12–13
psychologist 14

queen 17–18, 24–25

reincarnations 15

samurai 4
scientists 5
séance 12
shadow(s) 5, 23
ship 11
Society of Psychical
    Research 7
soldier(s) 8–9, 28
specter 22, 25
spiritualists 9

Tombstone, Arizona 22–23
Tower of London 16–17
trance 14

witnesses 5, 11, 17,
World War I 8–9
World War II 12